D1501777

Cram101 Textbook Outlines to accompany:

Truth, Lies and Advertising: The Art of Account Planning

Steel, 1st Edition

An Academic Internet Publishers (AIPI) publication (c) 2007.

You have a discounted membership at www.Cram101.com with this book.

Get all of the practice tests for the chapters of this textbook, and access in-depth reference material for writing essays and papers. Here is an example from a Cram101 Biology text:

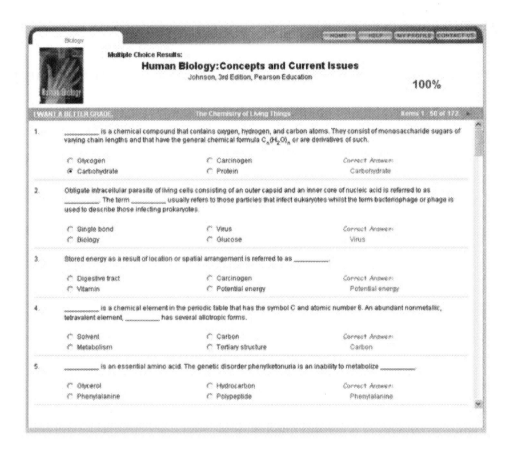

When you need problem solving help with math, stats, and other disciplines, www.Cram101.com will walk through the formulas and solutions step by step.

With Cram101.com online, you also have access to extensive reference material.

You will nail those essays and papers. Here is an example from a Cram101 Biology text:

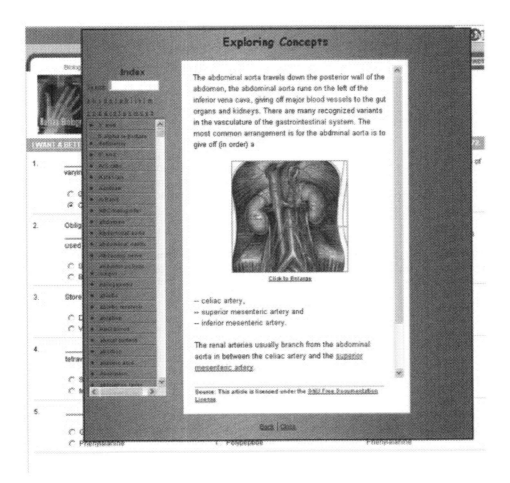

Visit **www.Cram101.com**, click Sign Up at the top of the screen, and enter DK73DW in the promo code box on the registration screen. Access to www.Cram101.com is normally $9.95, but because you have purchased this book, your access fee is only $4.95. Sign up and stop highlighting textbooks forever.

Learning System

Cram101 Textbook Outlines is a learning system. The notes in this book are the highlights of your textbook, you will never have to highlight a book again.

How to use this book. Take this book to class, it is your notebook for the lecture. The notes and highlights on the left hand side of the pages follow the outline and order of the textbook. All you have to do is follow along while your intructor presents the lecture. Circle the items emphasized in class and add other important information on the right side. With Cram101 Textbook Outlines you'll spend less time writing and more time listening. Learning becomes more efficient.

Cram101.com Online

Increase your studying efficiency by using Cram101.com's practice tests and online reference material. It is the perfect complement to Cram101 Textbook Outlines. Use self-teaching matching tests or simulate in-class testing with comprehensive multiple choice tests, or simply use Cram's true and false tests for quick review. Cram101.com even allows you to enter your in-class notes for an integrated studying format combining the textbook notes with your class notes.

Visit **www.Cram101.com**, click Sign Up at the top of the screen, and enter **DK73DW2131** in the promo code box on the registration screen. Access to www.Cram101.com is normally $9.95, but because you have purchased this book, your access fee is only $4.95. Sign up and stop highlighting textbooks forever.

Truth, Lies and Advertising: The Art of Account Planning
Steel, 1st

CONTENTS

Advertising	Advertising refers to paid, nonpersonal communication through various media by organizations and individuals who are in some way identified in the advertising message.
Points	Loan origination fees that may be deductible as interest by a buyer of property. A seller of property who pays points reduces the selling price by the amount of the points paid for the buyer.
Advertising agency	A firm that specializes in the creation, production, and placement of advertising messages and may provide other services that facilitate the marketing communications process is an advertising agency.
Guardian	A person to whom the law has entrusted the custody and control of the person, or estate, or both, of an incompetent person is a guardian.
Standing	Standing refers to the legal requirement that anyone seeking to challenge a particular action in court must demonstrate that such action substantially affects his legitimate interests before he will be entitled to bring suit.
Interest	In finance and economics, interest is the price paid by a borrower for the use of a lender's money. In other words, interest is the amount of paid to "rent" money for a period of time.
Prejudice	Prejudice is, as the name implies, the process of "pre-judging" something. It implies coming to a judgment on a subject before learning where the preponderance of evidence actually lies, or forming a judgment without direct experience.
Collaboration	Collaboration occurs when the interaction between groups is very important to goal attainment and the goals are compatible. Wherein people work together —applying both to the work of individuals as well as larger collectives and societies.
Expense	In accounting, an expense represents an event in which an asset is used up or a liability is incurred. In terms of the accounting equation, expenses reduce owners' equity.
Hearing	A hearing is a proceeding before a court or other decision-making body or officer. A hearing is generally distinguished from a trial in that it is usually shorter and often less formal.
Gain	In finance, gain is a profit or an increase in value of an investment such as a stock or bond. Gain is calculated by fair market value or the proceeds from the sale of the investment minus the sum of the purchase price and all costs associated with it.
Analogy	Analogy is either the cognitive process of transferring information from a particular subject to another particular subject (the target), or a linguistic expression corresponding to such a process. In a narrower sense, analogy is an inference or an argument from a particular to another particular, as opposed to deduction, induction, and abduction, where at least one of the premises or the conclusion is general.
Industry	A group of firms that produce identical or similar products is an industry. It is also used specifically to refer to an area of economic production focused on manufacturing which involves large amounts of capital investment before any profit can be realized, also called "heavy industry".
Target audience	That group that composes the present and potential prospects for a product or service is called the target audience.
Coupon	In finance, a coupon is "attached" to a bond, either physically (as with old bonds) or electronically. Each coupon represents a predetermined payment promized to the bond-holder in return for his or her loan of money to the bond-issuer. .
Context	The effect of the background under which a message often takes on more and richer meaning is a context. Context is especially important in cross-cultural interactions because some cultures are said to be high context or low context.
Yield	The interest rate that equates a future value or an annuity to a given present value is a yield.
Trust	An arrangement in which shareholders of independent firms agree to give up their stock in exchange for

trust certificates that entitle them to a share of the trust's common profits.

Premium	Premium refers to the fee charged by an insurance company for an insurance policy. The rate of losses must be relatively predictable: In order to set the premium (prices) insurers must be able to estimate them accurately.
Focus group	A small group of people who meet under the direction of a discussion leader to communicate their opinions about an organization, its products, or other given issues is a focus group.
Logo	Logo refers to device or other brand name that cannot be spoken.
Security	Security refers to a claim on the borrower future income that is sold by the borrower to the lender. A security is a type of transferable interest representing financial value.
Stock	In financial terminology, stock is the capital raized by a corporation, through the issuance and sale of shares.
Consideration	Consideration in contract law, a basic requirement for an enforceable agreement under traditional contract principles, defined in this text as legal value, bargained for and given in exchange for an act or promise. In corporation law, cash or property contributed to a corporation in exchange for shares, or a promise to contribute such cash or property.
Enterprise	Enterprise refers to another name for a business organization. Other similar terms are business firm, sometimes simply business, sometimes simply firm, as well as company, and entity.
Evaluation	The consumer's appraisal of the product or brand on important attributes is called evaluation.
Management	Management characterizes the process of leading and directing all or part of an organization, often a business, through the deployment and manipulation of resources. Early twentieth-century management writer Mary Parker Follett defined management as "the art of getting things done through people."
Marketing	Promoting and selling products or services to customers, or prospective customers, is referred to as marketing.
Supply	Supply is the aggregate amount of any material good that can be called into being at a certain price point; it comprises one half of the equation of supply and demand. In classical economic theory, a curve representing supply is one of the factors that produce price.
Illusion of control	Illusion of control is the tendency for human beings to believe they can control or at least influence outcomes of which researchers deem them to have no influence over.
Adoption	In corporation law, a corporation's acceptance of a pre-incorporation contract by action of its board of directors, by which the corporation becomes liable on the contract, is referred to as adoption.
Scientific method	The procedure for the systematic pursuit of knowledge involving the observation of facts and the formulation and testing of hypotheses to obtain theories, principles, and laws is called scientific method.
Authority	Authority in agency law, refers to an agent's ability to affect his principal's legal relations with third parties. Also used to refer to an actor's legal power or ability to do something. In addition, sometimes used to refer to a statute, case, or other legal source that justifies a particular result.
Users	Users refer to people in the organization who actually use the product or service purchased by the buying center.
Early adopters	Early adopters refers to the 13.5 percent of the population who are leaders in their social setting and act as an information source on new products for other people.
Household	An economic unit that provides the economy with resources and uses the income received to purchase goods and services that satisfy economic wants is called household.
Brand	A name, symbol, or design that identifies the goods or services of one seller or group of sellers and

	distinguishes them from the goods and services of competitors is a brand.
Advertising campaign	A comprehensive advertising plan that consists of a series of messages in a variety of media that center on a single theme or idea is referred to as an advertising campaign.
Union	A worker association that bargains with employers over wages and working conditions is called a union.
Production	The creation of finished goods and services using the factors of production: land, labor, capital, entrepreneurship, and knowledge.
Harmonization	Harmonization refers to the changing of government regulations and practices, as a result of an international agreement, to make those of different countries the same or more compatible.
Balance	In banking and accountancy, the outstanding balance is the amount of money owned, (or due), that remains in a deposit account (or a loan account) at a given date, after all past remittances, payments and withdrawal have been accounted for. It can be positive (then, in the balance sheet of a firm, it is an asset) or negative (a liability).
Precedent	A previously decided court decision that is recognized as authority for the disposition of future decisions is a precedent.
Tagline	A tagline is a variant of an advertising slogan typically used in movie marketing, commercials, and websites. The idea behind the concept is to create a memorable phrase that will sum up the tone and premise of a film, or to reinforce the subject's memory of a product or website.
Holder	A person in possession of a document of title or an instrument payable or indorsed to him, his order, or to bearer is a holder.
Competitor	Other organizations in the same industry or type of business that provide a good or service to the same set of customers is referred to as a competitor.
Holding	The holding is a court's determination of a matter of law based on the issue presented in the particular case. In other words: under this law, with these facts, this result.

Go to **Cram101.com** for the Practice Tests for this Chapter.
And, **NEVER** highlight a book again!

Assessment	Collecting information and providing feedback to employees about their behavior, communication style, or skills is an assessment.
Advertising	Advertising refers to paid, nonpersonal communication through various media by organizations and individuals who are in some way identified in the advertising message.
Interest	In finance and economics, interest is the price paid by a borrower for the use of a lender's money. In other words, interest is the amount of paid to "rent" money for a period of time.
Privilege	Generally, a legal right to engage in conduct that would otherwise result in legal liability is a privilege. Privileges are commonly classified as absolute or conditional. Occasionally, privilege is also used to denote a legal right to refrain from particular behavior.
Tactic	A short-term immediate decision that, in its totality, leads to the achievement of strategic goals is called a tactic.
Brand	A name, symbol, or design that identifies the goods or services of one seller or group of sellers and distinguishes them from the goods and services of competitors is a brand.
Industry	A group of firms that produce identical or similar products is an industry. It is also used specifically to refer to an area of economic production focused on manufacturing which involves large amounts of capital investment before any profit can be realized, also called "heavy industry".
Volkswagen	Volkswagen or VW is an automobile manufacturer based in Wolfsburg, Germany in the state of Lower Saxony. It forms the core of this Group, one of the world's four largest car producers. Its German tagline is "Aus Liebe zum Automobil", which is translated as "For the love of the car" - or, For Love of the People's Cars,".
Advertising agency	A firm that specializes in the creation, production, and placement of advertising messages and may provide other services that facilitate the marketing communications process is an advertising agency.
Brief	Brief refers to a statement of a party's case or legal arguments, usually prepared by an attorney. Also used to make legal arguments before appellate courts.
Distribution	Distribution in economics, the manner in which total output and income is distributed among individuals or factors.
Nielsen	When TV viewers or entertainment professionals in the United States mention "ratings" they are generally referring to Nielsen Ratings, a system developed by Nielsen Media Research to determine the audience size and composition of television programming. Nielsen Ratings are offered in over forty countries.
Driving force	The key external pressure that will shape the future for an organization is a driving force. The driving force in an industry are the main underlying causes of changing industry and competitive conditions.
Aid	Assistance provided by countries and by international institutions such as the World Bank to developing countries in the form of monetary grants, loans at low interest rates, in kind, or a combination of these is called aid. Aid can also refer to assistance of any type rendered to benefit some group or individual.
Market research	Market research is the process of systematic gathering, recording and analyzing of data about customers, competitors and the market. Market research can help create a business plan, launch a new product or service, fine tune existing products and services, expand into new markets etc. It can be used to determine which portion of the population will purchase the product/service, based on variables like age, gender, location and income level. It can be found out what market characteristics your target market has.

Restructuring	Restructuring is the corporate management term for the act of partially dismantling and reorganizing a company for the purpose of making it more efficient and therefore more profitable.
Marketing	Promoting and selling products or services to customers, or prospective customers, is referred to as marketing.
Market	A market is, as defined in economics, a social arrangement that allows buyers and sellers to discover information and carry out a voluntary exchange of goods or services.
Ad hoc	Ad hoc is a Latin phrase which means "for this purpose." It generally signifies a solution that has been tailored to a specific purpose and is makeshift and non-general, such as a handcrafted network protocol or a specific-purpose equation, as opposed to general solutions.
Account planner	Account planner refers to an outgrowth of British agency structure where a planner initiates and reviews research and participates in the creative process. In some agencies, the planner is considered a spokesperson for the consumer.
Contribution	In business organization law, the cash or property contributed to a business by its owners is referred to as contribution.
Portfolio	In finance, a portfolio is a collection of investments held by an institution or a private individual. Holding but not always a portfolio is part of an investment and risk-limiting strategy called diversification. By owning several assets, certain types of risk (in particular specific risk) can be reduced.
Front end	All the promotional activities that occur before a sale is made is a front end.
Trust	An arrangement in which shareholders of independent firms agree to give up their stock in exchange for trust certificates that entitle them to a share of the trust's common profits.
Agency shop	A place of employment where the employer may hire either labor union members or nonmembers, but where those who do not join the union must either pay union dues or donate an equivalent amount of money to a charity is called agency shop.
Profit	Profit refers to the return to the resource entrepreneurial ability; total revenue minus total cost.
Service	Service refers to a "non tangible product" that is not embodied in a physical good and that typically effects some change in another product, person, or institution. Contrasts with good.
Commission system	Commission system refers to a method of compensating advertising agencies whereby the agency receives a specified commission from the media on any advertising time or space it purchases.
Balance	In banking and accountancy, the outstanding balance is the amount of money owned, (or due), that remains in a deposit account (or a loan account) at a given date, after all past remittances, payments and withdrawal have been accounted for. It can be positive (then, in the balance sheet of a firm, it is an asset) or negative (a liability).
Prejudice	Prejudice is, as the name implies, the process of "pre-judging" something. It implies coming to a judgment on a subject before learning where the preponderance of evidence actually lies, or forming a judgment without direct experience.
Complement	A good that is used in conjunction with another good is a complement. For example, cameras and film would complement eachother.
Points	Loan origination fees that may be deductible as interest by a buyer of property. A seller of property who pays points reduces the selling price by the amount of the points paid for the buyer.

Correlation	A correlation is the measure of the extent to which two economic or statistical variables move together, normalized so that its values range from -1 to +1. It is defined as the covariance of the two variables divided by the square root of the product of their variances.
Argument	The discussion by counsel for the respective parties of their contentions on the law and the facts of the case being tried in order to aid the jury in arriving at a correct and just conclusion is called argument.
Nike	Because Nike creates goods for a wide range of sports, they have competition from every sports and sports fashion brand there is. Nike has no direct competitors because there is no single brand which can compete directly with their range of sports and non-sports oriented gear, except for Reebok.
Specie	Specie refers to coins, normally including only those made of precious metal.
Production	The creation of finished goods and services using the factors of production: land, labor, capital, entrepreneurship, and knowledge.
Hearing	A hearing is a proceeding before a court or other decision-making body or officer. A hearing is generally distinguished from a trial in that it is usually shorter and often less formal.
Foundation	A Foundation is a type of philanthropic organization set up by either individuals or institutions as a legal entity (either as a corporation or trust) with the purpose of distributing grants to support causes in line with the goals of the foundation.
Credit	Credit refers to a recording as positive in the balance of payments, any transaction that gives rise to a payment into the country, such as an export, the sale of an asset, or borrowing from abroad.
Focus group	A small group of people who meet under the direction of a discussion leader to communicate their opinions about an organization, its products, or other given issues is a focus group.
Gain	In finance, gain is a profit or an increase in value of an investment such as a stock or bond. Gain is calculated by fair market value or the proceeds from the sale of the investment minus the sum of the purchase price and all costs associated with it.
Context	The effect of the background under which a message often takes on more and richer meaning is a context. Context is especially important in cross-cultural interactions because some cultures are said to be high context or low context.
Security	Security refers to a claim on the borrower future income that is sold by the borrower to the lender. A security is a type of transferable interest representing financial value.
Partnership	In the common law, a partnership is a type of business entity in which partners share with each other the profits or losses of the business undertaking in which they have all invested.
American Marketing Association	The American Marketing Association is a professional association for marketers. It has approximately 38,000 members. It was formed in 1937 from the merger of two predecessor organizations.
Advertising campaign	A comprehensive advertising plan that consists of a series of messages in a variety of media that center on a single theme or idea is referred to as an advertising campaign.

Aid	Assistance provided by countries and by international institutions such as the World Bank to developing countries in the form of monetary grants, loans at low interest rates, in kind, or a combination of these is called aid. Aid can also refer to assistance of any type rendered to benefit some group or individual.
Advertising	Advertising refers to paid, nonpersonal communication through various media by organizations and individuals who are in some way identified in the advertising message.
Due diligence	Due diligence is the effort made by an ordinarily prudent or reasonable party to avoid harm to another party or himself. Failure to make this effort is considered negligence. Failure to make this effort is considered negligence.
Marketing	Promoting and selling products or services to customers, or prospective customers, is referred to as marketing.
Mistake	In contract law a mistake is incorrect understanding by one or more parties to a contract and may be used as grounds to invalidate the agreement. Common law has identified three different types of mistake in contract: unilateral mistake, mutual mistake, and common mistake.
Focus group	A small group of people who meet under the direction of a discussion leader to communicate their opinions about an organization, its products, or other given issues is a focus group.
Respondent	Respondent refers to a term often used to describe the party charged in an administrative proceeding. The party adverse to the appellant in a case appealed to a higher court.
Hearing	A hearing is a proceeding before a court or other decision-making body or officer. A hearing is generally distinguished from a trial in that it is usually shorter and often less formal.
Account planner	Account planner refers to an outgrowth of British agency structure where a planner initiates and reviews research and participates in the creative process. In some agencies, the planner is considered a spokesperson for the consumer.
Ad hoc	Ad hoc is a Latin phrase which means "for this purpose." It generally signifies a solution that has been tailored to a specific purpose and is makeshift and non-general, such as a handcrafted network protocol or a specific-purpose equation, as opposed to general solutions.
Common mistake	A common mistake is where both parties hold the same mistaken belief of the facts.
Insurance	Insurance refers to a system by which individuals can reduce their exposure to risk of large losses by spreading the risks among a large number of persons.
Broker	In commerce, a broker is a party that mediates between a buyer and a seller. A broker who also acts as a seller or as a buyer becomes a principal party to the deal.
Holder	A person in possession of a document of title or an instrument payable or indorsed to him, his order, or to bearer is a holder.
Policy	Similar to a script in that a policy can be a less than completely rational decision-making method. Involves the use of a pre-existing set of decision steps for any problem that presents itself.
Context	The effect of the background under which a message often takes on more and richer meaning is a context. Context is especially important in cross-cultural interactions because some cultures are said to be high context or low context.
Interest	In finance and economics, interest is the price paid by a borrower for the use of a lender's money. In other words, interest is the amount of paid to "rent" money for a period of time.
Industry	A group of firms that produce identical or similar products is an industry. It is also used specifically to refer to an area of economic production focused on manufacturing which involves large amounts of capital investment before any profit can be realized, also called

"heavy industry".

Extension	Extension refers to an out-of-court settlement in which creditors agree to allow the firm more time to meet its financial obligations. A new repayment schedule will be developed, subject to the acceptance of creditors.
Domestic	From or in one's own country. A domestic producer is one that produces inside the home country. A domestic price is the price inside the home country. Opposite of 'foreign' or 'world.'.
Specie	Specie refers to coins, normally including only those made of precious metal.
Brief	Brief refers to a statement of a party's case or legal arguments, usually prepared by an attorney. Also used to make legal arguments before appellate courts.
Preference	The act of a debtor in paying or securing one or more of his creditors in a manner more favorable to them than to other creditors or to the exclusion of such other creditors is a preference. In the absence of statute, a preference is perfectly good, but to be legal it must be bona fide, and not a mere subterfuge of the debtor to secure a future benefit to himself or to prevent the application of his property to his debts.
Trademark	A distinctive word, name, symbol, device, or combination thereof, which enables consumers to identify favored products or services and which may find protection under state or federal law is a trademark.
Recruitment	Recruitment refers to the set of activities used to obtain a sufficient number of the right people at the right time; its purpose is to select those who best meet the needs of the organization.
Incentive	An incentive is any factor (financial or non-financial) that provides a motive for a particular course of action, or counts as a reason for preferring one choice to the alternatives.
Brand	A name, symbol, or design that identifies the goods or services of one seller or group of sellers and distinguishes them from the goods and services of competitors is a brand.
Bond	Bond refers to a debt instrument, issued by a borrower and promising a specified stream of payments to the purchaser, usually regular interest payments plus a final repayment of principal.
Jargon	Jargon is terminology, much like slang, that relates to a specific activity, profession, or group. It develops as a kind of shorthand, to express ideas that are frequently discussed between members of a group, and can also have the effect of distinguishing those belonging to a group from those who are not.
Nike	Because Nike creates goods for a wide range of sports, they have competition from every sports and sports fashion brand there is. Nike has no direct competitors because there is no single brand which can compete directly with their range of sports and non-sports oriented gear, except for Reebok.
Global advertising	Global advertising refers to the use of the same basic advertising message in all international markets.
Utility	Utility refers to the want-satisfying power of a good or service; the satisfaction or pleasure a consumer obtains from the consumption of a good or service.
Argument	The discussion by counsel for the respective parties of their contentions on the law and the facts of the case being tried in order to aid the jury in arriving at a correct and just conclusion is called argument.
Channel	Channel, in communications (sometimes called communications channel), refers to the medium

used to convey information from a sender (or transmitter) to a receiver.

Consumption	In Keynesian economics consumption refers to personal consumption expenditure, i.e., the purchase of currently produced goods and services out of income, out of savings (net worth), or from borrowed funds. It refers to that part of disposable income that does not go to saving.
Market share data	A comparative measure that determines relative positions of firms in the marketplace is called market share data.
Market share	That fraction of an industry's output accounted for by an individual firm or group of firms is called market share.
Market	A market is, as defined in economics, a social arrangement that allows buyers and sellers to discover information and carry out a voluntary exchange of goods or services.
Trend	Trend refers to the long-term movement of an economic variable, such as its average rate of increase or decrease over enough years to encompass several business cycles.
Big Business	Big business is usually used as a pejorative reference to the significant economic and political power which large and powerful corporations (especially multinational corporations), are capable of wielding.
Advertising campaign	A comprehensive advertising plan that consists of a series of messages in a variety of media that center on a single theme or idea is referred to as an advertising campaign.
Positioning	The art and science of fitting the product or service to one or more segments of the market in such a way as to set it meaningfully apart from competition is called positioning.
Conspicuous consumption	Conspicuous consumption is a term introduced by the American economist and sociologist Thorstein Veblen, in The Theory of the Leisure Class (1899). It is used to describe the obvious consumption of goods, commodities and services for the sake of displaying income or wealth in order to acquire social status.
Appreciation	Appreciation refers to a rise in the value of a country's currency on the exchange market, relative either to a particular other currency or to a weighted average of other currencies. The currency is said to appreciate. Opposite of 'depreciation.' Appreciation can also refer to the increase in value of any asset.
Commodity	Could refer to any good, but in trade a commodity is usually a raw material or primary product that enters into international trade, such as metals or basic agricultural products.
Firm	An organization that employs resources to produce a good or service for profit and owns and operates one or more plants is referred to as a firm.
Fortune magazine	Fortune magazine is America's longest-running business magazine. Currently owned by media conglomerate Time Warner, it was founded in 1930 by Henry Luce. It is known for its regular features ranking companies by revenue.
Brand manager	A manager who has direct responsibility for one brand or one product line is called a brand manager.
Management	Management characterizes the process of leading and directing all or part of an organization, often a business, through the deployment and manipulation of resources. Early twentieth-century management writer Mary Parker Follett defined management as "the art of getting things done through people."
Competitor	Other organizations in the same industry or type of business that provide a good or service to the same set of customers is referred to as a competitor.
Dealer	People who link buyers with sellers by buying and selling securities at stated prices are

referred to as a dealer.

Regulation
Regulation refers to restrictions state and federal laws place on business with regard to the conduct of its activities.

Body language
Body language is a broad term for forms of communication using body movements or gestures instead of, or in addition to, sounds, verbal language, or other forms of communication.

Trial
An examination before a competent tribunal, according to the law of the land, of the facts or law put in issue in a cause, for the purpose of determining such issue is a trial. When the court hears and determines any issue of fact or law for the purpose of determining the rights of the parties, it may be considered a trial.

Jury
A body of lay persons, selected by lot, or by some other fair and impartial means, to ascertain, under the guidance of the judge, the truth in questions of fact arising either in civil litigation or a criminal process is referred to as jury.

Verdict
Usually, the decision made by a jury and reported to the judge on the matters or questions submitted to it at trial is a verdict. In some situations, however, the judge may be the party issuing a verdict.

Prejudice
Prejudice is, as the name implies, the process of "pre-judging" something. It implies coming to a judgment on a subject before learning where the preponderance of evidence actually lies, or forming a judgment without direct experience.

Forming
The first stage of team development, where the team is formed and the objectives for the team are set is referred to as forming.

Gain
In finance, gain is a profit or an increase in value of an investment such as a stock or bond. Gain is calculated by fair market value or the proceeds from the sale of the investment minus the sum of the purchase price and all costs associated with it.

Distribution
Distribution in economics, the manner in which total output and income is distributed among individuals or factors.

Evaluation
The consumer's appraisal of the product or brand on important attributes is called evaluation.

Layout
Layout refers to the physical arrangement of the various parts of an advertisement including the headline, subheads, illustrations, body copy, and any identifying marks.

Target audience
That group that composes the present and potential prospects for a product or service is called the target audience.

20

Go to **Cram101.com** for the Practice Tests for this Chapter.

Positioning	The art and science of fitting the product or service to one or more segments of the market in such a way as to set it meaningfully apart from competition is called positioning.
Advertising	Advertising refers to paid, nonpersonal communication through various media by organizations and individuals who are in some way identified in the advertising message.
Consideration	Consideration in contract law, a basic requirement for an enforceable agreement under traditional contract principles, defined in this text as legal value, bargained for and given in exchange for an act or promise. In corporation law, cash or property contributed to a corporation in exchange for shares, or a promise to contribute such cash or property.
Balance	In banking and accountancy, the outstanding balance is the amount of money owned, (or due), that remains in a deposit account (or a loan account) at a given date, after all past remittances, payments and withdrawal have been accounted for. It can be positive (then, in the balance sheet of a firm, it is an asset) or negative (a liability).
Research and development	The use of resources for the deliberate discovery of new information and ways of doing things, together with the application of that information in inventing new products or processes is referred to as research and development.
Service	Service refers to a "non tangible product" that is not embodied in a physical good and that typically effects some change in another product, person, or institution. Contrasts with good.
Prejudice	Prejudice is, as the name implies, the process of "pre-judging" something. It implies coming to a judgment on a subject before learning where the preponderance of evidence actually lies, or forming a judgment without direct experience.
Brief	Brief refers to a statement of a party's case or legal arguments, usually prepared by an attorney. Also used to make legal arguments before appellate courts.
Focus group	A small group of people who meet under the direction of a discussion leader to communicate their opinions about an organization, its products, or other given issues is a focus group.
Interest	In finance and economics, interest is the price paid by a borrower for the use of a lender's money. In other words, interest is the amount of paid to "rent" money for a period of time.
Nielsen	When TV viewers or entertainment professionals in the United States mention "ratings" they are generally referring to Nielsen Ratings, a system developed by Nielsen Media Research to determine the audience size and composition of television programming. Nielsen Ratings are offered in over forty countries.
Context	The effect of the background under which a message often takes on more and richer meaning is a context. Context is especially important in cross-cultural interactions because some cultures are said to be high context or low context.
Trust	An arrangement in which shareholders of independent firms agree to give up their stock in exchange for trust certificates that entitle them to a share of the trust's common profits.
Commodity	Could refer to any good, but in trade a commodity is usually a raw material or primary product that enters into international trade, such as metals or basic agricultural products.
Argument	The discussion by counsel for the respective parties of their contentions on the law and the facts of the case being tried in order to aid the jury in arriving at a correct and just conclusion is called argument.
Attachment	Attachment in general, the process of taking a person's property under an appropriate judicial order by an appropriate officer of the court. Used for a variety of purposes, including the acquisition of jurisdiction over the property seized and the securing of property that may be used to satisfy a debt.

Respondent	Respondent refers to a term often used to describe the party charged in an administrative proceeding. The party adverse to the appellant in a case appealed to a higher court.
Insurance broker	An insurance broker sources (brokes) contracts of insurance on behalf of their customers.The term Insurance Broker became a regulated term under the Insurance Brokers (Registration) Act 1977 which was designed to thwart the bogus practices of firms holding themselves as brokers but in fact acting as representative of one or more favoured insurance companies.
Insurance	Insurance refers to a system by which individuals can reduce their exposure to risk of large losses by spreading the risks among a large number of persons.
Broker	In commerce, a broker is a party that mediates between a buyer and a seller. A broker who also acts as a seller or as a buyer becomes a principal party to the deal.
Policy	Similar to a script in that a policy can be a less than completely rational decision-making method. Involves the use of a pre-existing set of decision steps for any problem that presents itself.
Security	Security refers to a claim on the borrower future income that is sold by the borrower to the lender. A security is a type of transferable interest representing financial value.
Investment	Investment refers to spending for the production and accumulation of capital and additions to inventories. In a financial sense, buying an asset with the expectation of making a return.
Industry	A group of firms that produce identical or similar products is an industry. It is also used specifically to refer to an area of economic production focused on manufacturing which involves large amounts of capital investment before any profit can be realized, also called "heavy industry".
Holding	The holding is a court's determination of a matter of law based on the issue presented in the particular case. In other words: under this law, with these facts, this result.
Honda	With more than 14 million internal combustion engines built each year, Honda is the largest engine-maker in the world. In 2004, the company began to produce diesel motors, which were both very quiet whilst not requiring particulate filters to pass pollution standards. It is arguable, however, that the foundation of their success is the motorcycle division.
Dealer	People who link buyers with sellers by buying and selling securities at stated prices are referred to as a dealer.
Toyota	Toyota is a Japanese multinational corporation that manufactures automobiles, trucks and buses. Toyota is the world's second largest automaker by sales. Toyota also provides financial services through its subsidiary, Toyota Financial Services, and participates in other lines of business.
Face value	The nominal or par value of an instrument as expressed on its face is referred to as the face value.
Points	Loan origination fees that may be deductible as interest by a buyer of property. A seller of property who pays points reduces the selling price by the amount of the points paid for the buyer.
Audit	An examination of the financial reports to ensure that they represent what they claim and conform with generally accepted accounting principles is referred to as audit.
Recession	A significant decline in economic activity. In the U.S., recession is approximately defined as two successive quarters of falling GDP, as judged by NBER.
Brand	A name, symbol, or design that identifies the goods or services of one seller or group of sellers and distinguishes them from the goods and services of competitors is a brand.

Appeal	Appeal refers to the act of asking an appellate court to overturn a decision after the trial court's final judgment has been entered.
Conspicuous consumption	Conspicuous consumption is a term introduced by the American economist and sociologist Thorstein Veblen, in The Theory of the Leisure Class (1899). It is used to describe the obvious consumption of goods, commodities and services for the sake of displaying income or wealth in order to acquire social status.
Consumption	In Keynesian economics consumption refers to personal consumption expenditure, i.e., the purchase of currently produced goods and services out of income, out of savings (net worth), or from borrowed funds. It refers to that part of disposable income that does not go to saving.
Confirmed	When the seller's bank agrees to assume liability on the letter of credit issued by the buyer's bank the transaction is confirmed.The term means that the credit is not only backed up by the issuing foreign bank, but that payment is also guaranteed by the notifying American bank.
Bond	Bond refers to a debt instrument, issued by a borrower and promising a specified stream of payments to the purchaser, usually regular interest payments plus a final repayment of principal.
Junk bond	In finance, a junk bond is a bond that is rated below investment grade. These bonds have a higher risk of defaulting, but typically pay high yields in order to make them attractive to investors.
BMW	BMW is an independent German company and manufacturer of automobiles and motorcycles. BMW is the world's largest premium carmaker and is the parent company of the BMW MINI and Rolls-Royce car brands, and, formerly, Rover.
Standing	Standing refers to the legal requirement that anyone seeking to challenge a particular action in court must demonstrate that such action substantially affects his legitimate interests before he will be entitled to bring suit.
Tangible	Having a physical existence is referred to as the tangible. Personal property other than real estate, such as cars, boats, stocks, or other assets.
Polaroid	The Polaroid Corporation was founded in 1937 by Edwin H. Land. It is most famous for its instant film cameras, which reached the market in 1948, and continue to be the company's flagship product line.
Trend	Trend refers to the long-term movement of an economic variable, such as its average rate of increase or decrease over enough years to encompass several business cycles.
Competitor	Other organizations in the same industry or type of business that provide a good or service to the same set of customers is referred to as a competitor.
Advertising campaign	A comprehensive advertising plan that consists of a series of messages in a variety of media that center on a single theme or idea is referred to as an advertising campaign.

Go to **Cram101.com** for the Practice Tests for this Chapter.

Brief	Brief refers to a statement of a party's case or legal arguments, usually prepared by an attorney. Also used to make legal arguments before appellate courts.
Writ	Writ refers to a commandment of a court given for the purpose of compelling certain action from the defendant, and usually executed by a sheriff or other judicial officer.
Advertising	Advertising refers to paid, nonpersonal communication through various media by organizations and individuals who are in some way identified in the advertising message.
Management	Management characterizes the process of leading and directing all or part of an organization, often a business, through the deployment and manipulation of resources. Early twentieth-century management writer Mary Parker Follett defined management as "the art of getting things done through people."
Account planner	Account planner refers to an outgrowth of British agency structure where a planner initiates and reviews research and participates in the creative process. In some agencies, the planner is considered a spokesperson for the consumer.
Analogy	Analogy is either the cognitive process of transferring information from a particular subject to another particular subject (the target), or a linguistic expression corresponding to such a process. In a narrower sense, analogy is an inference or an argument from a particular to another particular, as opposed to deduction, induction, and abduction, where at least one of the premises or the conclusion is general.
Advertising campaign	A comprehensive advertising plan that consists of a series of messages in a variety of media that center on a single theme or idea is referred to as an advertising campaign.
Balance	In banking and accountancy, the outstanding balance is the amount of money owned, (or due), that remains in a deposit account (or a loan account) at a given date, after all past remittances, payments and withdrawal have been accounted for. It can be positive (then, in the balance sheet of a firm, it is an asset) or negative (a liability).
Copywriter	Individual who helps conceive the ideas for ads and commercials and writes the words or copy for them is referred to as copywriter.
Manufacturing	Production of goods primarily by the application of labor and capital to raw materials and other intermediate inputs, in contrast to agriculture, mining, forestry, fishing, and services a manufacturing.
Context	The effect of the background under which a message often takes on more and richer meaning is a context. Context is especially important in cross-cultural interactions because some cultures are said to be high context or low context.
Sony	Sony is a multinational corporation and one of the world's largest media conglomerates founded in Tokyo, Japan. One of its divisions Sony Electronics is one of the leading manufacturers of electronics, video, communications, and information technology products for the consumer and professional markets.
Competitor	Other organizations in the same industry or type of business that provide a good or service to the same set of customers is referred to as a competitor.
Market	A market is, as defined in economics, a social arrangement that allows buyers and sellers to discover information and carry out a voluntary exchange of goods or services.
Technology	The body of knowledge and techniques that can be used to combine economic resources to produce goods and services is called technology.
Buyer	A buyer refers to a role in the buying center with formal authority and responsibility to select the supplier and negotiate the terms of the contract.
Tangible	Having a physical existence is referred to as the tangible. Personal property other than real

estate, such as cars, boats, stocks, or other assets.

Billboard	The most common form of outdoor advertising is called a billboard.
Assignment	A transfer of property or some right or interest is referred to as assignment.
Complexity	The technical sophistication of the product and hence the amount of understanding required to use it is referred to as complexity. It is the opposite of simplicity.
Policy	Similar to a script in that a policy can be a less than completely rational decision-making method. Involves the use of a pre-existing set of decision steps for any problem that presents itself.
Marketing	Promoting and selling products or services to customers, or prospective customers, is referred to as marketing.
Argument	The discussion by counsel for the respective parties of their contentions on the law and the facts of the case being tried in order to aid the jury in arriving at a correct and just conclusion is called argument.
Jargon	Jargon is terminology, much like slang, that relates to a specific activity, profession, or group. It develops as a kind of shorthand, to express ideas that are frequently discussed between members of a group, and can also have the effect of distinguishing those belonging to a group from those who are not.
Commodity	Could refer to any good, but in trade a commodity is usually a raw material or primary product that enters into international trade, such as metals or basic agricultural products.
Budget	Budget refers to an account, usually for a year, of the planned expenditures and the expected receipts of an entity. For a government, the receipts are tax revenues.
Dealer	People who link buyers with sellers by buying and selling securities at stated prices are referred to as a dealer.
Nissan	Nissan is Japan's second largest car company after Toyota. Nissan is among the top three Asian rivals of the "big three" in the US.
Industry	A group of firms that produce identical or similar products is an industry. It is also used specifically to refer to an area of economic production focused on manufacturing which involves large amounts of capital investment before any profit can be realized, also called "heavy industry".
Utility	Utility refers to the want-satisfying power of a good or service; the satisfaction or pleasure a consumer obtains from the consumption of a good or service.
Toyota	Toyota is a Japanese multinational corporation that manufactures automobiles, trucks and buses. Toyota is the world's second largest automaker by sales. Toyota also provides financial services through its subsidiary, Toyota Financial Services, and participates in other lines of business.
Brand	A name, symbol, or design that identifies the goods or services of one seller or group of sellers and distinguishes them from the goods and services of competitors is a brand.
Confirmed	When the seller's bank agrees to assume liability on the letter of credit issued by the buyer's bank the transaction is confirmed.The term means that the credit is not only backed up by the issuing foreign bank, but that payment is also guaranteed by the notifying American bank.
Focus group	A small group of people who meet under the direction of a discussion leader to communicate their opinions about an organization, its products, or other given issues is a focus group.
Respondent	Respondent refers to a term often used to describe the party charged in an administrative

Go to **Cram101.com** for the Practice Tests for this Chapter.

Go to **Cram101.com** for the Practice Tests for this Chapter.
And, **NEVER** highlight a book again!

	proceeding. The party adverse to the appellant in a case appealed to a higher court.
Trial	An examination before a competent tribunal, according to the law of the land, of the facts or law put in issue in a cause, for the purpose of determining such issue is a trial. When the court hears and determines any issue of fact or law for the purpose of determining the rights of the parties, it may be considered a trial.
Frequency	Frequency refers to the speed of the up and down movements of a fluctuating economic variable; that is, the number of times per unit of time that the variable completes a cycle of up and down movement.
Demographic	A demographic is a term used in marketing and broadcasting, to describe a demographic grouping or a market segment.
Appeal	Appeal refers to the act of asking an appellate court to overturn a decision after the trial court's final judgment has been entered.
Users	Users refer to people in the organization who actually use the product or service purchased by the buying center.
Household	An economic unit that provides the economy with resources and uses the income received to purchase goods and services that satisfy economic wants is called household.
Interest	In finance and economics, interest is the price paid by a borrower for the use of a lender's money. In other words, interest is the amount of paid to "rent" money for a period of time.
Gap	In December of 1995, Gap became the first major North American retailer to accept independent monitoring of the working conditions in a contract factory producing its garments. Gap is the largest specialty retailer in the United States.
Core	A core is the set of feasible allocations in an economy that cannot be improved upon by subset of the set of the economy's consumers (a coalition). In construction, when the force in an element is within a certain center section, the core, the element will only be under compression.
Polaroid	The Polaroid Corporation was founded in 1937 by Edwin H. Land. It is most famous for its instant film cameras, which reached the market in 1948, and continue to be the company's flagship product line.
Exchange	The trade of things of value between buyer and seller so that each is better off after the trade is called the exchange.
Logo	Logo refers to device or other brand name that cannot be spoken.
Nintendo	Nintendo has the reputation of historically being both the oldest intact company in the video game console market and one of the most influential and well-known console manufacturers, as well as being the most dominant entity in the handheld console market.
Tagline	A tagline is a variant of an advertising slogan typically used in movie marketing, commercials, and websites. The idea behind the concept is to create a memorable phrase that will sum up the tone and premise of a film, or to reinforce the subject's memory of a product or website.
Option	A contract that gives the purchaser the option to buy or sell the underlying financial instrument at a specified price, called the exercise price or strike price, within a specific period of time.
Stock	In financial terminology, stock is the capital raized by a corporation, through the issuance and sale of shares.
Distribution	Distribution in economics, the manner in which total output and income is distributed among

Go to **Cram101.com** for the Practice Tests for this Chapter.
And, **NEVER** highlight a book again!

individuals or factors.

Preference

The act of a debtor in paying or securing one or more of his creditors in a manner more favorable to them than to other creditors or to the exclusion of such other creditors is a preference. In the absence of statute, a preference is perfectly good, but to be legal it must be bona fide, and not a mere subterfuge of the debtor to secure a future benefit to himself or to prevent the application of his property to his debts.

Target audience

That group that composes the present and potential prospects for a product or service is called the target audience.

Aid

Assistance provided by countries and by international institutions such as the World Bank to developing countries in the form of monetary grants, loans at low interest rates, in kind, or a combination of these is called aid. Aid can also refer to assistance of any type rendered to benefit some group or individual.

34

Go to **Cram101.com** for the Practice Tests for this Chapter.

Sony	Sony is a multinational corporation and one of the world's largest media conglomerates founded in Tokyo, Japan. One of its divisions Sony Electronics is one of the leading manufacturers of electronics, video, communications, and information technology products for the consumer and professional markets.
Corporation	A legal entity chartered by a state or the Federal government that is distinct and separate from the individuals who own it is a corporation. This separation gives the corporation unique powers which other legal entities lack.
Account executive	The individual who serves as the liaison between the advertising agency and the client is the account executive. The account executive is responsible for managing all of the services the agency provides to the client and representing the agency's point of view to the client.
Marketing	Promoting and selling products or services to customers, or prospective customers, is referred to as marketing.
Advertising objectives	Those specific outcomes that are to be accomplished through advertising are referred to as advertising objectives.
Target audience	That group that composes the present and potential prospects for a product or service is called the target audience.
Advertising	Advertising refers to paid, nonpersonal communication through various media by organizations and individuals who are in some way identified in the advertising message.
Brief	Brief refers to a statement of a party's case or legal arguments, usually prepared by an attorney. Also used to make legal arguments before appellate courts.
Copywriter	Individual who helps conceive the ideas for ads and commercials and writes the words or copy for them is referred to as copywriter.
Advertising campaign	A comprehensive advertising plan that consists of a series of messages in a variety of media that center on a single theme or idea is referred to as an advertising campaign.
Nike	Because Nike creates goods for a wide range of sports, they have competition from every sports and sports fashion brand there is. Nike has no direct competitors because there is no single brand which can compete directly with their range of sports and non-sports oriented gear, except for Reebok.
Starbucks	Although it has endured much criticism for its purported monopoly on the global coffee-bean market, Starbucks purchases only 3% of the coffee beans grown worldwide. In 2000 the company introduced a line of fair trade products and now offers three options for socially conscious coffee drinkers. According to Starbucks, they purchased 4.8 million pounds of Certified Fair Trade coffee in fiscal year 2004 and 11.5 million pounds in 2005.
Mistake	In contract law a mistake is incorrect understanding by one or more parties to a contract and may be used as grounds to invalidate the agreement. Common law has identified three different types of mistake in contract: unilateral mistake, mutual mistake, and common mistake.
Complexity	The technical sophistication of the product and hence the amount of understanding required to use it is referred to as complexity. It is the opposite of simplicity.
Points	Loan origination fees that may be deductible as interest by a buyer of property. A seller of property who pays points reduces the selling price by the amount of the points paid for the buyer.
Consideration	Consideration in contract law, a basic requirement for an enforceable agreement under traditional contract principles, defined in this text as legal value, bargained for and given in exchange for an act or promise. In corporation law, cash or property contributed to a corporation in exchange for shares, or a promise to contribute such cash or property.

Go to **Cram101.com** for the Practice Tests for this Chapter.

Preference	The act of a debtor in paying or securing one or more of his creditors in a manner more favorable to them than to other creditors or to the exclusion of such other creditors is a preference. In the absence of statute, a preference is perfectly good, but to be legal it must be bona fide, and not a mere subterfuge of the debtor to secure a future benefit to himself or to prevent the application of his property to his debts.
Variable	A variable is something measured by a number; it is used to analyze what happens to other things when the size of that number changes.
Brand	A name, symbol, or design that identifies the goods or services of one seller or group of sellers and distinguishes them from the goods and services of competitors is a brand.
Principal	In agency law, one under whose direction an agent acts and for whose benefit that agent acts is a principal.
Interest	In finance and economics, interest is the price paid by a borrower for the use of a lender's money. In other words, interest is the amount of paid to "rent" money for a period of time.
Hierarchy	A system of grouping people in an organization according to rank from the top down in which all subordinate managers must report to one person is called a hierarchy.
Focus group	A small group of people who meet under the direction of a discussion leader to communicate their opinions about an organization, its products, or other given issues is a focus group.
Respondent	Respondent refers to a term often used to describe the party charged in an administrative proceeding. The party adverse to the appellant in a case appealed to a higher court.
Yield	The interest rate that equates a future value or an annuity to a given present value is a yield.
Quantitative research	Quantitative research is the systematic scientific investigation of quantitative properties and phenomena and their relationships. The objective of quantitative research is to develop and employ mathematical models, theories and hypotheses pertaining to natural phenomena. The process of measurement is central to quantitative research because it provides the fundamental connection between empirical observation and mathematical expression of quantitative relationships.
Evaluation	The consumer's appraisal of the product or brand on important attributes is called evaluation.
Clutter	The nonprogram material that appears in a broadcast environment, including commercials, promotional messages for shows, public service announcements, and the like is called clutter.
Argument	The discussion by counsel for the respective parties of their contentions on the law and the facts of the case being tried in order to aid the jury in arriving at a correct and just conclusion is called argument.
Senior management	Senior management is generally a team of individuals at the highest level of organizational management who have the day-to-day responsibilities of managing a corporation.
Management	Management characterizes the process of leading and directing all or part of an organization, often a business, through the deployment and manipulation of resources. Early twentieth-century management writer Mary Parker Follett defined management as "the art of getting things done through people."
Advertising agency	A firm that specializes in the creation, production, and placement of advertising messages and may provide other services that facilitate the marketing communications process is an advertising agency.
Context	The effect of the background under which a message often takes on more and richer meaning is a context. Context is especially important in cross-cultural interactions because some

Go to **Cram101.com** for the Practice Tests for this Chapter.

	cultures are said to be high context or low context.
Core	A core is the set of feasible allocations in an economy that cannot be improved upon by subset of the set of the economy's consumers (a coalition). In construction, when the force in an element is within a certain center section, the core, the element will only be under compression.
Investment	Investment refers to spending for the production and accumulation of capital and additions to inventories. In a financial sense, buying an asset with the expectation of making a return.
Pledge	In law a pledge (also pawn) is a bailment of personal property as a security for some debt or engagement.
Budget	Budget refers to an account, usually for a year, of the planned expenditures and the expected receipts of an entity. For a government, the receipts are tax revenues.
Market research	Market research is the process of systematic gathering, recording and analyzing of data about customers, competitors and the market. Market research can help create a business plan, launch a new product or service, fine tune existing products and services, expand into new markets etc. It can be used to determine which portion of the population will purchase the product/service, based on variables like age, gender, location and income level. It can be found out what market characteristics your target market has.
Negotiation	Negotiation is the process whereby interested parties resolve disputes, agree upon courses of action, bargain for individual or collective advantage, and/or attempt to craft outcomes which serve their mutual interests.
Market	A market is, as defined in economics, a social arrangement that allows buyers and sellers to discover information and carry out a voluntary exchange of goods or services.
Production	The creation of finished goods and services using the factors of production: land, labor, capital, entrepreneurship, and knowledge.
Innovation	Innovation refers to the first commercially successful introduction of a new product, the use of a new method of production, or the creation of a new form of business organization.
Gap	In December of 1995, Gap became the first major North American retailer to accept independent monitoring of the working conditions in a contract factory producing its garments. Gap is the largest specialty retailer in the United States.
Polaroid	The Polaroid Corporation was founded in 1937 by Edwin H. Land. It is most famous for its instant film cameras, which reached the market in 1948, and continue to be the company's flagship product line.
Parent company	Parent company refers to the entity that has a controlling influence over another company. It may have its own operations, or it may have been set up solely for the purpose of owning the Subject Company.
Tagline	A tagline is a variant of an advertising slogan typically used in movie marketing, commercials, and websites. The idea behind the concept is to create a memorable phrase that will sum up the tone and premise of a film, or to reinforce the subject's memory of a product or website.
Standing	Standing refers to the legal requirement that anyone seeking to challenge a particular action in court must demonstrate that such action substantially affects his legitimate interests before he will be entitled to bring suit.

Go to **Cram101.com** for the Practice Tests for this Chapter.

Preparation	Preparation refers to usually the first stage in the creative process. It includes education and formal training.
Advertising	Advertising refers to paid, nonpersonal communication through various media by organizations and individuals who are in some way identified in the advertising message.
Budget	Budget refers to an account, usually for a year, of the planned expenditures and the expected receipts of an entity. For a government, the receipts are tax revenues.
Consumption	In Keynesian economics consumption refers to personal consumption expenditure, i.e., the purchase of currently produced goods and services out of income, out of savings (net worth), or from borrowed funds. It refers to that part of disposable income that does not go to saving.
Per capita	Per capita refers to per person. Usually used to indicate the average per person of any given statistic, commonly income.
Commodity	Could refer to any good, but in trade a commodity is usually a raw material or primary product that enters into international trade, such as metals or basic agricultural products.
Industry	A group of firms that produce identical or similar products is an industry. It is also used specifically to refer to an area of economic production focused on manufacturing which involves large amounts of capital investment before any profit can be realized, also called "heavy industry".
Fund	Independent accounting entity with a self-balancing set of accounts segregated for the purposes of carrying on specific activities is referred to as a fund.
Advertising campaign	A comprehensive advertising plan that consists of a series of messages in a variety of media that center on a single theme or idea is referred to as an advertising campaign.
Forming	The first stage of team development, where the team is formed and the objectives for the team are set is referred to as forming.
Brief	Brief refers to a statement of a party's case or legal arguments, usually prepared by an attorney. Also used to make legal arguments before appellate courts.
License	A license in the sphere of Intellectual Property Rights (IPR) is a document, contract or agreement giving permission or the 'right' to a legally-definable entity to do something (such as manufacture a product or to use a service), or to apply something (such as a trademark), with the objective of achieving commercial gain.
Advertising agency	A firm that specializes in the creation, production, and placement of advertising messages and may provide other services that facilitate the marketing communications process is an advertising agency.
Marketing	Promoting and selling products or services to customers, or prospective customers, is referred to as marketing.
Complement	A good that is used in conjunction with another good is a complement. For example, cameras and film would complement eachother.
Focus group	A small group of people who meet under the direction of a discussion leader to communicate their opinions about an organization, its products, or other given issues is a focus group.
Respondent	Respondent refers to a term often used to describe the party charged in an administrative proceeding. The party adverse to the appellant in a case appealed to a higher court.
Incentive	An incentive is any factor (financial or non-financial) that provides a motive for a particular course of action, or counts as a reason for preferring one choice to the alternatives.

Convergence	The blending of various facets of marketing functions and communication technology to create more efficient and expanded synergies is a convergence.
Hearing	A hearing is a proceeding before a court or other decision-making body or officer. A hearing is generally distinguished from a trial in that it is usually shorter and often less formal.
Media plan	A document consisting of objectives, strategies, and tactics for reaching a target audience through various media vehicles is a media plan.
Dayparts	Dayparts refer to the time segments into which a day is divided by radio and television networks and stations for selling advertising time.
Stock	In financial terminology, stock is the capital raized by a corporation, through the issuance and sale of shares.
Billboard	The most common form of outdoor advertising is called a billboard.
Precedent	A previously decided court decision that is recognized as authority for the disposition of future decisions is a precedent.
Conversion	Conversion refers to any distinct act of dominion wrongfully exerted over another's personal property in denial of or inconsistent with his rights therein. That tort committed by a person who deals with chattels not belonging to him in a manner that is inconsistent with the ownership of the lawful owner.
Mass media	Mass media refers to non-personal channels of communication that allow a message to be sent to many individuals at one time.
Closing	The finalization of a real estate sales transaction that passes title to the property from the seller to the buyer is referred to as a closing. Closing is a sales term which refers to the process of making a sale. It refers to reaching the final step, which may be an exchange of money or acquiring a signature.
Nestle	Nestle is the world's biggest food and beverage company. In the 1860s, a pharmacist, developed a food for babies who were unable to be breastfed. His first success was a premature infant who could not tolerate his own mother's milk nor any of the usual substitutes. The value of the new product was quickly recognized when his new formula saved the child's life.
General Mills	In 2001, the General Mills purchased Pillsbury, although it was officially described as a "merger." While many of the Pillsbury-branded products are still manufactured by General Mills, some products had to be sold off to allow the merger since the new company would have held a very strong monopoly position.
Promotion	Promotion refers to all the techniques sellers use to motivate people to buy products or services. An attempt by marketers to inform people about products and to persuade them to participate in an exchange.
Nabisco	In 2000 Philip Morris Companies acquired Nabisco; that acquisition was approved by the Federal Trade Commission subject to the divestiture of products in five areas: three Jell-O and Royal brands types of products (dry-mix gelatin dessert, dry-mix pudding, no-bake desserts), intense mints (such as Altoids), and baking powder. Kraft later purchased the company.
Brand	A name, symbol, or design that identifies the goods or services of one seller or group of sellers and distinguishes them from the goods and services of competitors is a brand.
Household	An economic unit that provides the economy with resources and uses the income received to purchase goods and services that satisfy economic wants is called household.
Confirmed	When the seller's bank agrees to assume liability on the letter of credit issued by the

buyer's bank the transaction is confirmed.The term means that the credit is not only backed up by the issuing foreign bank, but that payment is also guaranteed by the notifying American bank.

Interest

In finance and economics, interest is the price paid by a borrower for the use of a lender's money. In other words, interest is the amount of paid to "rent" money for a period of time.

Merchandising

Merchandising refers to the business of acquiring finished goods for resale, either in a wholesale or a retail operation.

Tangible

Having a physical existence is referred to as the tangible. Personal property other than real estate, such as cars, boats, stocks, or other assets.

Go to **Cram101.com** for the Practice Tests for this Chapter.
And, **NEVER** highlight a book again!

9 781428 809994